Original title:
Petals in the Breeze

Author: Sophia Kingsley
ISBN HARDBACK: 978-1-80567-033-9
ISBN PAPERBACK: 978-1-80567-113-8

Playful Currents of Beauty

Tiny dancers swirl and sway,
Tickled by the wind's ballet.
They giggle in a colorful flight,
Sprinkling laughter, pure delight.

With whispers soft, they encourage cheer,
Flipping hats when friends come near.
Their games create a fragrant spree,
As they tease the busy bee.

Oh look! A swirl of hues invade,
Chasing clouds, not one afraid.
In the air, they tease and twirl,
A silly, fragrant, happy whirl.

The sun's a spotlight, laughter peals,
An ode to joy, the breeze reveals.
Nature's giggles softly play,
With every gust, embrace the day.

The Artistry of Wind-Kissed Flora

A canvas brushed with colors wild,
Nature's mischief, nature's child.
They laugh and frolic, side by side,
As gusts of laughter gently glide.

Wind throws a party, here they go,
Jumping high, putting on a show.
A twist, a turn, in fancy flight,
Swaying through the morning light.

Each bloom a friend, a jolly mate,
Linking arms, they celebrate.
With petals bright, they spin and cheer,
In this bouquet, there's no fear.

The breeze tickles with giggly grace,
A playful, flowery, joyous place.
In every nook, where laughter grows,
Where whimsy dances, beauty glows.

Where the Wildflowers Roam Free

In a field where daisies dance,
Bees wear tiny pants.
Buttercups giggle as they prance,
While ants organize a chance.

Grasshoppers leap with glee,
Singing songs of jubilee.
Ladybugs play hide and seek,
A silly game, so to speak.

The sun shines down with flair,
Tickling toes without a care.
Nature's laughter fills the air,
As flowers wear their brightest wear.

Ribbons of Color in Motion

Swirling shades in a playful race,
Colors chase in a lively space.
Breezes toss them with a grin,
A wild swirl where giggles begin.

A red one trips on a blue,
They laugh, oh what a view!
Yellow's twirl spins to amaze,
While green just shimmies in a daze.

The wind is a cheeky tease,
Tugging and pulling with such ease.
As ribbons of warmth take flight,
Nature’s pranks bring pure delight.

A Lament for Lost Fragrance

Oh, sweet smell of lemon zest,
Why did you leave our little fest?
Daisies plot to bring you back,
While violets dance with a lack.

With chocolate blooms, we conspire,
To lure you with sweet desire.
But scents escape like sneaky cats,
While roses gossip about the rats.

Lavender dreams float away,
Whispers of what used to stay.
A fragrant ghost, forever missed,
In gardens full of fragrant twist.

Stories Carried with the Ebb

Oh, how the whispers ride the wind,
Tales of flowers that have sinned.
A daffodil fell for a bee,
But he was sweet on a cherry tree.

The river chuckled, smooth and sly,
As yellow blooms waved goodbye.
They carried stories, oh so bold,
Of sunshine days and nights of gold.

With every tide that comes and goes,
A new adventure always flows.
Laughing leaves share secrets near,
While petals spill their tales sincere.

Whispers of Blooming Softness

A flower sneezed, oh what a sight,
It sent its neighbors off in flight.
Their vibrant hues went twirling fast,
Like playful kids in spring, they laughed.

One rosy bud wore shades of gray,
Claimed it was stylish for the day.
A daisy winked, said, "You're absurd!"
As bees flew past, they simply heard.

A tulip danced in morning light,
With petals swirling, took to flight.
It tripped on grass, a silly blunder,
And fell with grace, it laughed in wonder.

The whole bouquet began to scheme,
To prank the wind, it seemed a dream.
With giggles soft and colors bright,
They teased the sky until the night.

Dancing Fragments of Nature

A breeze blew in, oh what a tease,
It rapped the buds like playful bees.
They spun around in dizzy glee,
Whispering jokes, oh can't you see?

The violets planned a waltz today,
But tripped on roots, they lost their way.
The sunflowers laughed, their necks so tall,
As blooms collided, they had a ball.

Lily called out, “Catch me if you can!”
The petals flew like a busy fan.
They twirled in circles, skipping past,
With giggles bright, they danced, they laughed.

Each stem a jester in green attire,
Conspiring with the winds, oh so dire.
In lively colors, antics unfurled,
Nature's jesters, the silliest world.

Flight of the Floral Whispers

A marigold took off in style,
With silly hops, and a big wide smile.
It wished to fly, so up it went,
To float on air, quite accidentally spent.

The daisies watched, eyes opened wide,
As their brave friend took a bumpy ride.
It swerved and dipped, a comic show,
Like a clumsy dancer in offbeat flow.

The roses giggled, “What a thrill!”
As the winds played tricks, it froze, then spilled.
All the blooms joined in the spree,
And tumbled down, that's how they’d be.

With laughter loud, they made a pact,
To soar once more, for fun and act.
On wings of joy, the colors swayed,
In their floral dance, the world displayed.

Gentle Flurries of Color

A fluffy cloud, the blooms conspired,
To toss their colors, oh how admired.
With a burst of pink and dashes bright,
They turned the garden into surreal light.

“Oh dear!” cried out a timid fern,
As the petals danced in a fun-filled churn.
They tickled bees and swayed on high,
While butterflies were buzzing by.

A crocus slipped, it went too far,
Landed soft on a passing car.
The driver laughed, a sight so sweet,
As petals bowed in their silly feat.

With each small gust, the giggles hummed,
Colors swirled as laughter bummed.
In nature's mischief, joy laid claim,
In every whisper, a silly name.

Drifting Hues of Tomorrow

Colors flutter, a playful glance,
Nature's dance in a quirky trance.
Whispers giggle, the leaves unwind,
In this chaos, joy we find.

Sunshine tickles the tips of trees,
A squirrel stumbles, oh what a tease!
Laughter echoes, the world’s a jest,
Tomorrow's hues are dressed in zest.

Softening under the Sun

Buds relax as the sun goes down,
Overcome by warmth, they start to frown.
A cheeky breeze steals their positions,
Wiggling out like garden magicians.

Grasshoppers chirp in a merry band,
Can't the flowers take a stand?
But they sway and sway in a funny pose,
Feeling lazy, like they're garden pros.

A Romance of Graceful Ephemera

In the garden, a silly love spins,
Fleeting moments dance on whims.
Butterflies flirt, oh what a sight,
Chasing each other till dark meets light.

One blooms high, the other dips low,
A romantic joke in nature's show.
They giggle as petals start to collide,
Spreading the laughter, nowhere to hide.

Embraces Between the Breeze

A gentle hug from the cheeky air,
Caresses flowers with wild flair.
They laugh together, a joyous pair,
Swirling giggles, floating everywhere.

The wind whispers secrets, oh so sly,
Who knew nature could be quite spry?
In this frolic, the world feels light,
As breezy friends share pure delight.

Driftwood of Nature's Canvas

Once a stick, now a fancy zoom toy,
Floating downstream, it thinks it's a buoy.
With a flick and a splash, it's part of the scene,
A wooden explorer where water is queen.

It drifts past the lilies, gives frogs quite a fright,
Pretending it's slick like it's ready for flight.
But all the wet antics can't hide its true aim,
Just looking for friends in nature's grand game.

Cadence of the Wandering Willow

A willow with gossip that sways in the wind,
Tells tales of the squirrels and the bees that have sinned.
With branches a-flutter, it dances for fun,
While critters beneath giggle, ‘til their day’s done.

“Have you seen the oak? Stiff as a board!”
It chuckles aloud, giving roots quite the hoard.
Fluffy clouds listen, trying not to laugh,
As this leaf-laden diva takes nature's own path.

The Scent of Forgotten Skies

A whiff of the past floats on a warm breeze,
It smells like old socks mixed with honey and cheese.
Clouds above chuckle, while the sun rolls its eyes,
As memories tumble like soft butterfly sighs.

“Oh, what a riot!” the old barn owl hoots,
While the days dance by in their mismatched boots.
Each scent brings a giggle from corners unseen,
Life's juicy aromas, odd yet pristine.

Swaying Colors of the Meadow

In a field where hues giggle and play,
Flowers are dancing as bugs bust a sway.
Yellow and purple, they swap silly tales,
While grass tickles ankles, and sunlight prevails.

"Oh, what a day to be all dressed up!"
Shouted the daisies, while filling their cup.
With laughter and whispers on colorful wings,
The meadow's a party with joy that it brings.

A Flutter Through Golden Hours

In the park, a flower fights,
Worn by days and sunny bites.
It flops and flutters, what a show,
Like a dancer, to and fro.

Bees giggle as they buzz on by,
"Who's that one with awkward style?"
The stem bends low, then springs up high,
"I'm just here to make you smile!"

A sunbeam pokes around the bend,
The flower rolls, it has no end.
With a twist and a casual sway,
It greets the folks on holiday.

Laughing daisies join the dance,
With wind as partner, they enhance.
Petal pals, their laughter loud,
Underneath a leafy shroud.

Echoes of Floral Daydreams

A tulip told a daffodil,
"I think I've caught a funny chill!"
They shook and rattled, what a scene,
Among the greens, like silly beans.

The sun looks down, gives them a wink,
"You two are more than flowers, I think!"
With every gust, they start to giggle,
Their laughter flows, a joyful wiggle.

A bumblebee joined in the fun,
"With pollen on my back, I run."
They shrugged and said, "Come dance with us!"
The garden spills with endless fuss.

Together, they whirl, a merry crew,
In petal hats of every hue.
For in this patch of floral cheer,
Funny moments last all year.

Softly Unfurled Tresses

A bloom with curls, a fancified day,
Spins in circles, not one little sway.
"Watch me twirl!" it calls out loud,
As leaves giggle, forming a crowd.

A dandelion, puffy and bright,
Blows its fluff with all its might.
"Catch me if you can!" it shouts,
As the breeze laughs, dancing about.

A sunflower with big, floppy ears,
Bobs along, staving off fears.
"I'm the tallest, look at me shine!"
Its friends reply, "Just give it time!"

With wind as host, they dance along,
Swaying whimsically to the song.
In fields of colors, laughter drums,
As joys of floral life just hums.

The Wind's Gentle Caress

A breezy fellow, sly and spry,
Tickles blooms as they wave hi.
"Hey there, petals, let's have some fun!"
With every gust, they leap and run.

A rose bud blushed, all pink and neat,
Commented with a giggle so sweet,
"If you think you can ruffle me,"
"I'll show you how wild I can be!"

A clover sneezed, oh what a sight,
Caught the wind in mid-flight.
"Oops! Excuse me!" it laughed with glee,
As butterflies danced joyously.

The wind, a prankster, swirled around,
In gardens where joy can be found.
Together they rise, they tumble, they spin,
Creating a world where fun's the win.

Laughter of the Wandering Petals

A flower lost its way today,
It danced upon a sunny ray.
With every twist, it gave a wink,
And giggled soft, what do you think?

The wind declared a silly race,
It spun around with funny grace.
The daisies cheered, they joined the fun,
As petals leapt, a wild run!

In search of cakes with icing sweet,
They flipped and flopped on dainty feet.
Oh look, a bee with shades so bright,
It buzzed along, a comical sight!

At dusk they sighed and flopped to rest,
A flower's life, it’s quite the jest.
With laughter ringing through the night,
Another day will bring delight!

Gossamer Memories of Spring

Once upon a time, a bloom,
Decided it could leave the gloom.
It twirled and skipped like little Mike,
And tripped on grass—oh what a spike!

The clouds all chuckled, sky so blue,
As petals formed a wobbly crew.
They giggled loud, 'We're free, hooray!'
And danced like children in a play.

A butterfly, quite posh and neat,
Challenged them to skip and cheat.
But flowers, bold and full of cheer,
Just laughed and shouted, "Come down here!"

With memories sweet, they'll never fade,
These silly tales of blossoms made.
Tomorrow's laughs are in the air,
So let them dance without a care!

Odyssey of the Whirling Blossoms

A swirl of blooms began to prance,
In search of a most glorious dance.
The wind chuckled, swirled them around,
As giggles echoed through the ground.

They wiggled past a garden gnome,
Who scowled at them—oh, let’s not roam!
But flowers laughed, their colors bright,
They continued on their silly flight.

A tulip shouted, “Let’s play tag!”
And off they went, an epic wag.
Through buttercups and clover fields,
Their laughter soared as joy it yields!

Soon twilight fell, their trails aglow,
With memories of glee in tow.
Tomorrow's mischief waits ahead,
For wandering blooms and tales unsaid!

Transient Kisses from Nature

A breeze swung low, with laughter laced,
It tickled flowers, joy embraced.
With cheeks of pink and yellow hues,
They giggled loud, with playful muse.

"Come join our squabble, what a show!"
Cried violets with a cheeky glow.
They turned and twisted, spun with glee,
As dandelions danced, "Count to three!"

But just like that, the moment flew,
And petals tumbled, "Oh, boo-hoo!"
Yet with each twist, there's laughter sweet,
A nature's jest, oh what a treat!

In morning's light, they felt the tease,
Of transient fun in the gentle breeze.
With whispers soft and giggles bright,
They courted joy, their hearts in flight!

Breezy Secrets of the Heart

A dandelion whispers a wish,
As it twirls from a child's little fist.
“Will it fly far? Will it escape?
Maybe land on a dog with a cape!”

The butterflies giggle in secret too,
Plotting their mischief, a prank to undo.
They tickle the noses of flowers so proud,
Who sneeze in protest, shouting out loud!

The tulips are blushing, they’re quite bashful,
They hide their giggles in petals so colorful.
“A snail just slipped on a sunny-day grin,
His shell launched him off like a wobbly spin!”

Then a breeze bursts forth with laughter and cheer,
With every puff, it spreads joy far and near.
Unruly secrets in gardens abound,
Where silly surprises and giggles are found.

Harmonies of the Wistful Garden

Scenes of a garden with tunes so absurd,
The tulips hum softly, they sing like a bird.
"Lowest note hits!" cries a funky petunia,
"A bumblebee's buzzing, let's change the tune, yeah!"

The marigolds dance with their petals in pairs,
Swapping their colors like fashionable wares.
"I'd love to wear yellow!" one daisy declares,
But only if green doesn't give her unfair shares.

A sunbeam slips in, causing quite the ruckus,
A shadowy beetle thinks he's quite the focus.
"I'm structuring sunlight, I'm leading this team!"
And chairs of bright petals erupt in a dream!

All critters are buzzing, forming a band,
As plants sway and giggle, can you understand?
The harmonies echo, a silly delight,
In gardens where laughter and whimsy take flight.

When Colors Take Flight

Once a yellow rose tried to tango with blue,
But ended up twirling with a breeze that flew.
"I'm not getting dizzy!" it cried through the spin,
As violets watched with a sly little grin.

The sunflowers shouted, "Let's start a parade!"
As petals marched forth, swinging colors displayed.
A poppy dressed bold gave a wink to a fern,
"Can you catch my glitter? It's your turn to earn!"

A rainbow appeared, it was bending in glee,
"I'm here to assist! Who needs harmony?"
The daisies were laughing, unable to stand,
As colors collided, a whimsical band.

So blossoms and blooms crafted giggles galore,
While the wind swayed them all to their whims as they soar.
Colors were flying, it was all quite a sight,
A fest of the floral, oh what pure delight!

Kisses from the Sunlit Petals

Sunshine peeked through, just like a prankster,
Tickling all petals, the ultimate jester.
One flower exclaimed with a glow on its face,
"I've got sunshine lotion, who needs space?"

A daisy declared with a giddy little hop,
"Who ordered this breeze? When will it stop?"
As twirling rose buds shot confetti of dew,
And bees headed straight to the party, all flew!

The pansies competed for who's brightest of all,
While lilacs just giggled, refusing to fall.
"A kiss from the sun! Just see my bold flair,
What's warmer than petals that dance in the air?"

The garden erupted in giggles and glee,
While sunshine confirmed it was all meant to be.
Kisses were traded in whimsical ways,
In a sun-drenched garden, where laughter stays!

Celestial Ribbons of Light

In the garden, a party is set,
Bees in tuxedos, you bet!
Daisies giggle, tulips sway,
While the sun spills lemonade, hooray!

Butterflies wear their finest attire,
Flapping about, never tire.
A daffodil drops her hat in glee,
Saying, "Join my dance, come, let it be!"

A worm winks, sporting a tie so bright,
As the lilies chuckle, what a sight!
They twirl in joy under the sky,
With a wink and a nod, oh my!

So, raise your glass to this floral spree,
Where petals laugh in jubilee.
Nature's circus, all in good fun,
Under the watchful eye of the sun!

A Gentle Kiss from Afar

From high above, clouds glance down,
Spotting a daisy in a crown.
"Oh dear flower, how you shine!"
Spoke a cloud, feeling quite divine.

The daisy blushed, oh what a scene,
"Your fluff makes me feel like a queen!"
Wind whispered tales of love so great,
While the blades of grass giggled at fate.

A rose chimed in, quite the charmer,
"Dear cloud, don't be such a farmer!"
For bees and blooms danced in delight,
As pollen twirled in the warm sunlight.

In this garden of comedy, we find,
Funny romances of every kind.
Leaves shake with laughter; nature's jest,
A kiss from afar, oh what a fest!

Secrets Shared Among the Flowers

Whispers float among the buds,
"Did you see how the lily shrugged?"
Roses giggle, what a tease,
Sharing secrets on the breeze.

“Oh darling, your perfume is strong,
But you must know where you belong!"
Daisies giggle, butterflies chuckle,
As petals sway in this flower huddle.

A sunflower confessed with a grin,
"I spy a bee with a crooked pin!"
Delightful chaos, what a scene,
In their world of smirks, all serene.

Amidst the gossip, laughter and glee,
The flowers bond, so wild and free.
In the sun's warm glow, they revel,
In this garden's chatter, they all settle!

Glimmers of an Unseen Dance

Under the moon, a twinkle so rare,
Flowers gather for the midnight fair.
With glimmers bright, they sway as one,
Inviting the stars to join in fun.

A lavender led the all-star parade,
While marigolds curtsied, unafraid.
Crickets played their tunes so sweet,
As blooms tapped their roots to the beat.

“Hey there, rose, show us your style,
Bend and sway, make us all smile!”
Said a lilac, blushing with glee,
As the night wore on, wild and free.

What a night, with laughter and dance,
In the garden’s glow, they took a chance.
For beneath the stars, they found their song,
In this unseen dance where they belong!

The Lullaby of Dancing Flora

In the garden, flowers sway,
Bumping into plants that play.
A daisy laughs, a rose just twirls,
While marigolds spin 'round like whirls.

Chasing bees with silly spins,
Tickling winds, they share their grins.
“Catch me if you can!” they call,
As breezes brush and gently fall.

Whimsical Whispers Beyond Reach

A dandelion giggles, all aglow,
Playing hide-and-seek with a flower foe.
"I'm here, I'm not!" it teases with glee,
While the tulips just chuckle and leave it be.

Laughter floats on the summer air,
As butterflies prance without a care.
"Come on, join us!" the violets sing,
Ticklish petals, what joy they bring!

Nature's Gentle Serenade

A breeze tickles the leaves, they quack,
While the sunbeams play in a bright green pack.
Together they dance, with hops and skips,
Fluffy clouds chuckle, puffing their lips.

The trees hold hands—what a sight to see!
Trying to dance, all wiggly and free.
"Oops! I tripped," whispers a shy limb,
As the earth roars back in a playful hymn.

A Tapestry of Aerial Dreams

Each leaf a jester, each flower a knight,
Together they joke in the soft sunlight.
Swaying with laughter, they tickle the sky,
With whimsy and giggles that float oh so high.

A robin chirps out a funny old tune,
As the daisies bob like they've had too much moon.
A comical clash, a floral parade,
Nature's own jesters, in colors displayed!

Sunlit Blooms and Silken Winds

Bouncing flowers in the sun,
Chasing bees that seem to run.
Whispering secrets, oh so sly,
Tickling noses as they fly.

Dancing lightly, bright and bold,
Waving stories yet untold.
Butterflies in fancy dress,
Laughing at the blooms' finesse.

Sun-kissed petals throw a party,
Jokes exchanged, a bit so hearty.
Goldfinches chirp with comic flair,
As pollen drifts through fragrant air.

With each gale, a giggle swells,
Nature's laughter, sweet spell it tells.
Joyful hues of every shade,
A riot where the garden's played.

Fragrant Dreams on the Horizon

In a garden where the sun beams,
Flowers burst with fragrant dreams.
Bouncing breezes tease and shout,
Scaring gnomes, they twist about.

Whimsical scents float around,
Wiggly worms dance on the ground.
Sneezy petals laugh so loud,
While shy daisies hide in a crowd.

Horizon sings with vibrant hues,
Jokesters in nature, sharing views.
Tulips giggle, roses beam,
Nature's side-splitter team!

They poke fun at spring’s sweet cheer,
With each flutter, joy draws near.
Chasing whims with every gust,
In laughter and blooms, we trust.

Whirlwinds of Soft Embrace

Twisting softly, swirling dance,
Flowers twirl in bright romance.
Garlands laugh and bridesmaids play,
While squirrels plot a wild foray.

Breezes tickle every face,
Joyful giggles fill the space.
Nature's chaos sways with ease,
As bloom-boats sail on the breeze.

Dandelions take to air,
As if they're free, without a care.
Silly seeds with dreams of flight,
They befriend the playful night.

Whirlwinds spin, the garden shouts,
In this chaos, laughter sprouts.
Tiny acorns join the fun,
While nature winks, the joy's begun.

Fleeting Echoes of Spring

Echoes crackle through the trees,
Flowers dance with utmost ease.
Springtime jokes float on the air,
Leaves join in with lively flair.

Each blossom hums a silly tune,
Tickling toes beneath the moon.
Lavender laughs with sweet delight,
While daisies tumble in the night.

In this romp of colors bright,
Every turn brings pure delight.
Buttercups with giggly grace,
Join a wacky flower chase.

Fleeting moments, nature's jest,
In every bloom, a raucous fest.
Breezy whispers, fun's not far,
As spring dances, our twinkling star.

Serenade of Fluttering Blooms

In the garden, flowers dance,
Wobbling like a squirrel's prance,
Bees are buzzing 'round the way,
Sipping nectar, making play.

Butterflies in silly flight,
Chasing shadows left and right,
With a giggle, blooms take a spin,
What a day, let spring begin!

Colors clash, a sight absurd,
Roses mumble, not a word,
Daisies chuckle, petals sway,
What a joke, the sun's here to stay!

With the wind, all flowers toss,
Playing games, a funny gloss,
In this wacky, wild display,
Even clouds seem prone to play!

Soft Murmurs of Springtime

Whispers in the air take flight,
Lilies giggle, oh what a sight,
Tulips sneezing, what a scene,
Daffodils in bright, gold sheen.

Buttercups play peek-a-boo,
Hiding from the morning dew,
A chorus of laughter plays,
Every stem in cheerful rays.

Bumblebees in quirky spin,
Buzzing tales of where they've been,
Charming blooms with witty tease,
Nature's stage, such silly ease.

As the breeze tickles the green,
Life's a riddle, sweet and keen,
Joyful jests in flower's dress,
Springtime's humor, nothing less!

Enchanted Drift of Blossoms

Pansies prance in fanciful fun,
Bobbing heads, oh aren't they spun?
Tulips giggle, swaying by,
In this garden circus high!

The violets throw a dance-off,
Petal twirls, a joyous scoff,
Daisies wink with sunny grace,
In each bloom, a smiling face.

Chasing breezes, whims ignite,
Every flower’s pure delight,
With petals bright and laughter shared,
Nature’s jokes are fully aired.

Oh, the way they sway and flop,
Never wanting this to stop,
In this merry floral scheme,
Life’s a flower-filled dream!

Caravan of Floral Sighs

Here comes the parade of blooms,
With each one, enchantment looms,
Daisy chimes and rose bouquet,
Frolicking through the sunny day.

Laughter spills from every stem,
Chortles rise in floral hem,
Jestful roses, teasing all,
As they bounce and spin and sprawl.

Sunflowers in a friendly tug,
Playful as a warm, bright mug,
Carnivals of color burst,
Flora fancies, wild and cursed.

Caravans of joy on the move,
Silly blooms in a happy groove,
Join the fun, don't be shy,
In this flower-filled levity, fly!

Nature’s Gentle Crescendo

In a forest where squirrels dance,
Fungi wear hats, if given a chance.
The wind whispers secrets, oh so sly,
While raccoons debate if they can fly.

Sunbeams giggle, tickle the ground,
A rabbit hops, his ears so round.
Bees in tutus buzz to the beat,
As flowers sway with dainty feet.

Lizards practicing yoga pose,
Chasing shadows, they strike a pose.
Butterflies waltz in the sunlit space,
While a snail bags about winning the race.

Nature’s laughter fills the air,
Even the ants catch a breath of flare.
Misfits make up the troupe of cheer,
As trees applaud with branches near.

A Symphony of Falling Hues

Leaves tumble down in a dizzy swirl,
A squirrel sighs, “My acorn! Oh, pearl!”
The colors clash like a paint fight,
While birds mimic pop stars, oh, what a sight!

A cat on a branch looks mighty pleased,
At her little kingdom, totally ungrieved.
“Do I look like a queen?” she thinks with a grin,
As a mischievous chipmunk sneaks in for the win.

Clouds congest in a fluffy debate,
Who rolls in fast, who’s fashionably late?
All join the party, the sky’s a delight,
While raindrops play tag, oh what a sight!

The sun’s a DJ, spinning real fun,
Making shadows groove 'til the day is done.
Nature’s concert, loud and absurd,
With laughter and love whispered among the herd.

The Language of Shimmering Leaves

Rustling whispers between the boughs,
“Who made your hat?!” the magic vows.
A leaf laughs back, “It’s just my style!”
As bugs hold a meeting, each critter a smile.

Caterpillars argue in colorful hues,
“Mine’s more fabulous!” “No, yours needs a muse!”
They gossip and giggle, with much clever flair,
As the breeze catches tales in mid-air.

A ladybug struts with her polka-dot pride,
Sipping on dew like a cocktail guide.
“Oops!” she exclaims, “Just spilt on the floor!”
While ants clean up, “Just don’t dive in more!”

Wind chimes rattle in comical glee,
As trees join the dance, wild and free.
Nature’s own gossip, alive with the sound,
In this leafy theater, joy knows no bound.

Tender Moments Adrift

Dandelions float like tiny clouds,
They giggle and whisper, gathering crowds.
A breeze sweeps by, the seeds take flight,
“Catch me if you can!” they shout in delight.

A dog in a hat makes his rounds,
Wagging his tail while spinning in bounds.
With a stick in his mouth, he prances with glee,
As frogs join the chorus, croaking, “Yippee!”

A baby owl blinking, watching the fun,
While rabbits play hopscotch under the sun.
“Who’s next? Who’s next?” they laugh, full of cheer,
As butterflies flutter, saying, “We’re here!”

Each moment is silly, a magical sight,
With laughter that sparkles, oh so bright!
So grab a wildflower, enjoy the parade,
Nature’s sweet laughter, a grand charade!

Delicate Journeys Through the Air

A dandelion drifts with flair,
Wobbling like it just don't care.
It twirls and spins, a little dance,
Hey, look at me! I took a chance!

Up and away, oh what a sight,
Floating free, oh what a flight.
Landed on a dog's wet nose,
And poof! No one even knows!

The Ballad of Swaying Blooms

There once was a flower with a funny face,
Trying to run in a wild race.
It slipped on dew, oh what a fall,
It giggled loud, like it had it all.

A bee buzzed in to say hello,
"Watch out, my friend, that's not the flow!"
But the bloom just laughed, with great delight,
I'm the fastest in this garden light!

Echoes of Nature’s Life

In the wind, whispers start to play,
A leaf jokes, 'Today’s my day!'
It spins around like it’s on a trip,
And lands on a cat—oh, what a flip!

The tree’s got rhythm, sways to a tune,
Shaking its branches under the moon.
“Dance with me!” it shouts with glee,
Who knew trees could be so funny?

Curved Pathways of Light

Bumbles of light twist and twirl,
Nature's way of giving a whirl.
A laughing sunbeam danced on a shoe,
"Why shine alone? Come, dance too!"

A rainbow joined, with a cheeky grin,
"Who's up for a laugh? Let's all spin!"
With giggles and wiggles, they twinkled bright,
Turning the world into sheer delight!

Secrets Carried on the Air

A ticklish wind blew by my ear,
Whispering jokes only I could hear.
It carried giggles, light and spry,
As dandelions danced and flew high.

Silly secrets swirled in flight,
Turning frowns into pure delight.
I chased a laugh like a rolling ball,
Only to trip—oh, not at all!

A butterfly, in polka dots dressed,
Flew by and put my giggles to test.
With a wink, it caused a great stir,
As I fell, it mocked with a purr.

Who knew the sky held such wonder?
With each sweet laugh, we pulled the thunder.
While trees joined in, dancing their dance,
As laughter throbbed, we took our chance.

Wandering Blooms at Dusk

In the twilight glow, blooms took to flight,
Twirling and twisting, a hilarious sight.
One sunflower slipped, tripping on dew,
“Catch me if you can!” it giggled, it's true.

The daisies formed a conga line,
With winks and nudges, they did just fine.
A bee in shades strutted around,
“Buzz off!” it laughed, “I’m party-bound!”

Tulips tried to hula, oh so loud,
While giggling grass blades cheered, so proud.
“Oh, how we wished for more time to play!”
As the dusk sun blushed, then faded away.

Yet every petal danced like they knew
That tomorrow's fun would bloom anew.
With laughter painting the evening hue,
Who knew plants loved silly just like we do?

Cherished Moments in Flight

Look at the daisies, so full of glee,
Spinning around like they're at a spree.
A gust lifts them without a care,
"Freeze your petals!" a lilac would dare.

I once saw a rose trying to twirl,
With petals flailing like a curly whirl.
"Don't be shy!" the violets would say,
As each bloom joined in a ballet.

The air was thick with silliness spread,
As bumbles and laughs filled every thread.
Chasing each other, oh what a chase,
In this floral frolic, we found our place.

When all were gathered, a giggle parade,
Together they blossomed, their fears displayed.
Let's cherish the moments, fleeting and bright,
For each laugh shared is a pure delight.

Colors on the Whispering Wind

Colorful whispers float by my head,
A rainbow of chuckles, it's truly widespread.
Marigolds giggled, their orange so bold,
Telling tales of mischief we've yet to unfold.

"Oh look!" cried the pansies, "a patch of fun!"
As butterflies chased till the day was done.
With colors aflutter, it turned into play,
The breeze frolicked and carried them away.

Lavenders winked as they swayed to the beat,
With each little turn, they danced on their feet.
An iris proclaimed, "I'm the best in the field!"
As laughter erupted, no secrets concealed.

So let's paint the sky with hues of delight,
For every bloom shares a giggle in flight.
Together they flourish, never alone,
In this mix of colors, we've happily grown.

Where Blossoms Meet the Sky

Up above, where flowers dance,
A squirrel steals a daisy's chance.
He wears it like a fancy hat,
While bees buzz loud: "What's up with that?"

Nectar flows like gossip shared,
Dandelions look quite unprepared.
They puff and laugh, they sway and bend,
In this topsy-turvy trend!

A bumblebee in a tuxedo neat,
Tries to charm a lady sweet.
But all she does is roll her eyes,
And zips off quick amidst the skies!

Each bloom a giggle, every leaf a jest,
Nature's party is quite the fest.
Laughter floats on wings so light,
In a garden bursting with delight!

Interlude at Summer’s Edge

A butterfly with mismatched socks,
Flutters by while teasing flocks.
"Do you think I look so fab?"
The flowers giggle, give a jab.

A grasshopper hops on a beat,
Plays the tambourine with his feet.
Frogs join in with croaks and croons,
They serenade beneath the moons.

A cat sits snoozing, dreams awry,
While sunbeams tickle, oh my, oh my!
In pools of laughter, shadows play,
As summer whispers, "Stay! Don’t stray!"

Each moment sparkles, shines anew,
In this wacky world, all askew.
With smiles spread from sun to sun,
The edge of summer’s just begun!

Gliding Through Imagined Worlds

On wings of whimsy, dreams can soar,
Past candy clouds and chocolate shores.
A snail in shades sips lemonade,
As jellybeans invade the glade.

A duck in boots struts down the lane,
Dancing ‘round in the summer rain.
While fireflies flash their little lights,
Sharing secrets of starry nights.

This realm of giggles, twirls, and spins,
Where laughter's tangled in silly grins.
Even the daisies join the fun,
Thinking life's a race to run!

With every turn, a chuckle's found,
In this world where joy abounds.
Imagination paints the skies,
With colors of laughter, oh, how time flies!

Visions on a Breath of Wind

Whispers twirl like a funny tune,
As kites unfurl beneath the moon.
A cactus dreams of being round,
While hedgehogs wonder, “Where's the sound?”

In a waltz with gusts, they shake and slide,
A troupe of daisies, wild and wide.
Their giggles echo on puffs of air,
As bubblegum clouds begin to flare.

A ladybug, with spots so bright,
Finds herself in a dance with light.
She twirls and spins in red and black,
While ants declare, “Oh, look at that!”

Oh, the joy of breezy sights,
Where silly tales take flight in heights.
With every gust, a secret shared,
In this whimsical world, all dared!

Elysium of Windborne Beauty

The flowers twirl a dance so grand,
They spin and sway, a floral band.
A bee gets stuck in tangled grace,
It bumps and jiggles, what a race!

A daffodil in yellow bright,
Winks at the sky, such a funny sight.
The wind plays tag, what a bold tease,
As petals tumble with utmost ease.

A tulip trips over daisies' toes,
Giggles erupt as laughter flows.
In this garden where whimsy reigns,
Funny faces sprout from the lanes.

In every gust, joy takes its flight,
Nature's jest, a sheer delight.
So let us cheer, and we shall sing,
For in this dance, we find our spring.

Ephemeral Colors on the Current

Floating colors, quite a sight,
Can you spot the rogue spright?
A rosey rogue leaps with glee,
While dandelions laugh, so free.

The breeze sweeps in, with a playful shove,
A marigold's hat flies, oh love!
It bounces off a bumble's head,
That must have been quite a thread!

Around the park, it flits like a tease,
Colors chase, oh what a breeze!
With petals swirling, laughter's call,
Nature’s jesters, the best of all.

Let’s join this merry, vibrant race,
And make some silly, flowery face.
For every gust that comes to play,
Brings joy to brighten up the day.

Blossoms' Lullaby in Motion

A flower's nap turns out to be,
An unexpected jubilee.
Sleeping softly, it starts to dance,
In the wind's soft, playful prance.

A fragrant jester on a spree,
Twirling round a jolly bee.
With every turn, a slight hiccup,
In the breeze, they share a cup.

Silly flowers, you're in a whirl,
Making faces, giving a twirl.
Petal giggles fly through the air,
Bringing joy everywhere.

So close your eyes and take a chance,
Let nature's dreams lead to a prance.
In this lullaby, laughter's sweet,
A blooming world, a rhythmic beat.

Mirth of the Wandering Fragrance

The scent of spring gets caught in glee,
It tickles noses, oh whoopee!
A whiff of laughter sneaks around,
As blossoms chuckle without a sound.

Pollen's parade on a breezy ride,
Sneezes erupt, can't even hide!
A fun mishap, a floral joke,
Nature giggles as smiles invoke.

A daisy dons a petal hat,
Winking at a snoozing cat.
In every whiff, joy blooms anew,
For laughter's scent is pure and true.

The stroll through fields becomes a glee,
As fragrance dances wild and free.
So join the fun, there's much to share,
In this fragrant comedy, beyond compare.

The Symphony of Floating Flowers

In the fields where colors sway,
A clumsy bee took flight today.
It zoomed past blooms with quite a flair,
But tangled hard in fragrant hair.

The daisies giggled in delight,
As petals danced, they took to flight.
A squirrel laughed upon a branch,
His acorn dropped—a crazy chance!

A butterfly, with bright attire,
Caught in a wind, spun like a flyer.
It fluttered round, a dizzy swirl,
While daisies formed a twirling whirl.

And all around, the flowers cheer,
For nature’s mischief draws us near.
With giggles soft, they sway and sway,
In this absurd, floral ballet.

Secrets Carried on the Wind

A whisper blew from flower to flower,
It tickled leaves at twilight hour.
The secrets shared were not so grand,
Just who could swing the best, they planned.

A tulip teased a shy old rose,
“Your fragrance? Say, it's just for show!”
But soon a breeze blew wild and free,
And caught them in a shimmy spree.

They swayed and spun, a flow'ry fight,
Compliments, they flung in flight.
“Your color’s bright, but can you dance?”
The daisies laughed, “Give it a chance!”

As petals twirled with carefree grace,
All grumpy blooms were gone without a trace.
With laughter carried on the gale,
Each floral heart began to pale.

Tapestry of Fragile Dreams

A daisy dreamed to fly so high,
But tangled up, she asked the sky,
"Would you grant me wings, oh please?
Or at least help me catch that breeze?"

A rose replied with playful cheer,
"Just twirl around, and never fear!"
She spun in place, a dizzy kick,
Then fell flat—that was the trick!

In giggles soft, the flowers joked,
As dandelions popped and poked.
"Your dreams are fine, my fragile friend,
But how to rise, you've yet to spend!"

So here they swayed, in laughter bound,
In dreams and giggles, joy was found.
A tapestry of hopes on show,
In every breeze, their laughter flowed.

A Parade of Delicate Hues

On the path, a line so bright,
With every shade, it felt just right.
A parade formed in jolly line,
With flowers dancing, feeling fine.

The violets strutted, bold and brave,
While pansies wiggled, mischief wave.
"My hue is best!" a tulip cried,
But giggles sparked the joyful ride.

A sunflower led with golden beams,
As petals twirled in happy dreams.
Giggling flowers all in a rush,
With laughter loud, there's never hush.

The bumblebees joined in with cheer,
As the blossoms spun without a fear.
A festive sight, this colorful bunch,
A wondrous way to greet the lunch!

The Fairies' Return from the Meadow

Tiny wings flutter, with giggles in tow,
They've danced in the flowers, put on quite a show.
In lantern light laughter, they sprinkle their charms,
Watch out for the mischief, it comes with their farms.

They steal all the sweets and hide them away,
While toasting with nectar, they sing and they play.
On daisies they skip, with such sprightly delight,
Who knew that such trouble could come from their flight?

They tickle the daisies, a butterfly's tease,
Creating ruckus like bees in the trees.
With every soft landing and fluttering cheer,
You'd swear that the garden just brewed some good beer!

So if you see shadows where nothing is found,
It's just those wee fairies dancing around.
With giggly exploits, they merrily prance,
Stealing your snacks while they swing and they dance.

Dreams Embraced by Dandelion Seeds

A fluffy white wish, with a puff and a blow,
They scatter like laughter, in bright summer glow.
The kids try to catch them, a wild little chase,
But seeds just fly faster, in their airy race.

Each one a small dream, or so they declare,
As they tumble and twirl, scattering with flair.
But don't be too swift, or you'll ruin the fun,
'Cause catching a wish isn't easily done!

They float through the air, like confetti of white,
But watch out my friend, on a windy night.
For one tiny tickle, and you'll sneeze—ACHOO!
And there go your dreams, how rude of the zoo!

What once was a wish, is now pollen and dust,
Yet laughter still lingers, it's part of the trust.
In gardens of giggles, and whims that don't cease,
We're rolling with laughter, oh come, let's release!

Fantasies Unfurling in Flight

A flight of bright colors, they spin and they sway,
Imaginations soar, as they whirl from the clay.
With antics and capers, they frolic and tease,
Like pixies in sneakers, they do as they please.

A butterfly lands, and shouts out with glee,
"Hey, join in my dance, be friends with me!"
But all of the flowers are giggling too loud,
As grasses all whisper, 'Hey, look at this crowd!'

The ladybugs laugh, with their tiny round spots,
As crunching in leaves makes the funniest thoughts.
Each puff of the dandelion tickles the air,
A burst of soft giggles, good luck if you dare!

So let your dreams flutter as high as they can,
In whimsical paths, a fantastical plan.
With wings like confetti, they glide through each night,
In a world full of jest, they take playful flight.

The Music of the Floral Wind

The breeze plays a tune, on the petals so sly,
With whispers and chuckles that drift rather high.
It tickles the roses, gives daisies a grin,
Turns quiet to raucous, let the fun begin!

As the sun sets in bows and the day starts to sleep,
The flowers all gather, their secrets to keep.
In a circle they waltz, with roots in a twist,
And giggle about how the wind made them missed!

A sunflower shimmies, while prone to good cheer,
While tulips debate, which one’s the best beer.
Oh, the music of laughter and rustling leaves,
An orchestra blooming in what nature weaves!

So if you’re ever wandering slow through the glade,
Just listen to whispers, where fun never fades.
The wind sings a story, its notes full of glee,
In the grandest of concerts, come take a seat, see!

Cascade of Nature's Lullabies

A flower sneezed and lost a friend,
The bee just chuckled, on the mend.
With every bloom, there comes a giggle,
A dance of petals, watch them wiggle.

Squirrels in hats, they've gathered round,
Sharing jokes with roots and ground.
A dandelion, in high spirits,
Sways like it's found the best of lyrics.

The wind then laughed, with a gentle tease,
Spinning flowers like a game of freeze.
Who knew nature had its jest?
Laughter's bloom, a grand little fest.

As night descends, the fun won't fade,
Moonlit whispers in a parade.
Flora chuckles in their naps,
Sleeping flowers, giggling zaps.

Vignettes of the Floating Garden

In a garden, where giggles grow,
Flowers tell stories, side by side, flow.
A daffodil dressed in yellow bright,
Jokes with marigolds, what a sight!

Two tulips dancing in a line,
Bouncing softly, sipping sunshine.
A ladybug joins with a twirl,
What a sneaky, playful swirl!

Violets whisper, "Did you hear?
The roses spilled their tea, oh dear!"
Petunias chime in with a wink,
"It's all just petals, what do you think?"

As day turns dim, laughter fills the air,
With all the flora, dancing with flair.
A waltz of leaves, soft and spry,
In nature's playground, spirits fly.

The Journey of the Awakened Flora

Morning dew brings giggles near,
Flowers wake, spreading cheer.
"Did you see a cloud today?
It looked like popcorn, come what may!"

Hydrangeas shiver, sharing dreams,
"Life's but a joke, or so it seems."
Sunflowers chuckle, faces wide,
"Keep on smiling, take it in stride!"

A snail with swagger creeps along,
Making friends with ferns, soft as song.
"Don't rush," he said, with a sly grin,
"Life's a race, but I'll just spin!"

As whispers flutter and laughter flies,
The garden's secrets capture the skies.
With every moment, joy is found,
In the harmony of the ground.

Kaleidoscope of Floral Moments

A tulip wore a bowtie bright,
While daisies giggled in pure delight.
"Who's got the best bloom?" they debated,
"Mine's got flair, yours is outdated!"

In this realm where laughter swirls,
Each flower flirts and lightly twirls.
"Where's the party?" a rose proclaimed,
"Here's a secret, and then we named!"

Carnations blushed, oh such affair,
As butterflies danced without a care.
They spun and twirled, in gentle tease,
"Catch me if you can," a playful breeze.

Moonlight wraps this comedy show,
With secret whispers, soft and low.
Each petal holds a tale so grand,
In this garden, laughter's unplanned!

A Ballet of Colors in the Air

A flower dressed in yellow hat,
Twirls around, and then goes splat!
The sky giggles in bright delight,
As blossoms dance in pure sunlight.

A purple bloom slips on a shoe,
And twirls like dancers, oh, so few!
The daisies chuckle, 'What a sight!'
As petals whirl like chums in flight.

A gentle breeze, a twist and turn,
A tulip shouts, "Hey, watch me burn!"
But all it does is lightly sway,
And blush all pink, in its ballet.

Petals hop on spring's warm ride,
Making jokes that they can’t hide.
They plan a gig, a flower show,
With laughter echoing below.

Breath of Spring Awakening

A daffodil sneezes, 'Achoo!'
And sprinkles pollen on a shoe.
With laughter shared among the crew,
The blooms arise, confirm it's true!

'Time to awake, let’s spread the cheer!"
Said tulips blooming, loud and clear.
They laugh at winter, what a snooze!
As rainbows pop in vivid hues.

The petals tumble, roll, and flip,
While sipping nectar from a sip.
In spring, they know it’s not a race,
Just fun and frolic, a bright embrace!

They face the sun with laughter grand,
As bumblebees join in the band.
What joy to dance, to sway in change,
In every gust, there's something strange!

Shadows of Blossoms on the Ground

On the sidewalk, flowers dance,
Their shadows play, a wild romance.
A wind's chuckle, a bug's delight,
A flower's hat takes a sudden flight.

Bees wear sunglasses, sipping tea,
Ants in tuxedos, quite a sight to see.
They plot a picnic, oh so grand,
Yet tumble down, can't take a stand.

The daisies giggle, make a fuss,
While dandelions take the bus.
With every sway, they're full of glee,
As laughter lifts them, wild and free.

So if you stroll beneath the sun,
With floral pals, you'll have such fun.
Join the dance, it's pure, no doubt,
In shadowed hues, life's a laugh-out-loud.

The Playful Spirit of Summer

Summer swirls in funky hats,
Frogs wear shades and do backflats.
Lemonade stands, a buzzing hive,
Sipping joy, the world alive.

Pineapple laughs, a fruity cheer,
Sun's warm hugs, they draw us near.
Flip-flops squeak on sandy toes,
With every wave, a new pose flows.

Picnics tossed, but ants invade,
With tiny carts, a joyful parade.
A frisbee flies, in mid-air spins,
Only to land where chaos begins.

Fireflies spark in evening hues,
Crickets play tunes, the summer blues.
Every moment, a joyful tease,
In the season’s humor, we find our ease.

Explorations of Whispering Gardens

In a garden where whispers glow,
Squirrels gossip, putting on a show.
The roses giggle, coats of pink,
While tulips chat, they hardly blink.

A snail in glasses reads a book,
While ants on bicycles take a look.
Butterflies clown, they dance and zoom,
Turning the garden into a room.

With sun's bright laughter, flowers spin,
A veggie race to see who'll win.
Tomatoes tumble on a lawn of green,
In this funny scene, life feels serene.

So in this patch of humor and glee,
Let's join the laughter, wild and free.
For hidden magic's found with ease,
Among these blooms that tease the breeze.

The Journey Beyond the Norm

In a world where daisies sing,
A hippo waves from a rubber ring.
Journey forth with a sunflower hat,
To a realm where laughter's where it's at.

Unicorns race on pogo sticks,
While turtles tell their funniest tricks.
The moon plays hopscotch, a wild scene,
Turned topsy-turvy in summer’s sheen.

Every road is a twisty bend,
With trees that giggle and flowers that blend.
Painted clouds in a rainbow flight,
Bringing joy from morn till night.

So grab a friend, let’s wander wide,
In quirky lands where fun’s our guide.
For life’s a ride, so take the turn,
In this good cheer, let’s laugh and learn.

www.ingramcontent.com/pod-product-compliance
Lightning Source LLC
Chambersburg PA
CBHW071835160426
43209CB00003B/308
9781805670339